TOOLS FOR CAREGIVERS

- **F&P LEVEL:** C
- **WORD COUNT:** 46
- **CURRICULUM CONNECTIONS:** senses, tastes, adjectives

Skills to Teach

- **HIGH-FREQUENCY WORDS:** a, I, it, my, they, we, with
- **CONTENT WORDS:** eat, cake, candy, chips, cracker, lemon, pickle, salty, sour, sweet, taste(s), tongue, yum
- **PUNCTUATION:** exclamation point, periods
- **WORD STUDY:** long /e/, spelled ea (eat); long /e/, spelled ee (sweet); long /e/, spelled y (candy, salty); /ow/, spelled ou (sour)
- **TEXT TYPE:** information report

Before Reading Activities

- Read the title and give a simple statement of the main idea.
- Have students "walk" through the book and talk about what they see in the pictures.
- Introduce new vocabulary by having students predict the first letter and locate the word in the text.
- Discuss any unfamiliar concepts that are in the text.

After Reading Activities

Flip back through the book. Ask the readers what the foods in the book taste like. Explain that sour, salty, and sweet are all adjectives. They describe, or tell us, how something tastes. Write each adjective on the board. Can readers name other foods or beverages that taste sour, salty, or sweet? Under each adjective, write their answers on the board.

Tadpole Books are published by Jump!, 5357 Penn Avenue South, Minneapolis, MN 55419, www.jumplibrary.com

Copyright ©2023 Jump. International copyright reserved in all countries. No part of this book may be reproduced in any form without written permission from the publisher.

Editor: Jenna Gleisner **Designer:** Emma Bersie

Photo Credits: Picture Partners/Shutterstock, cover; maxpro/Shutterstock, 1; Jade Albert Studio, Inc./Getty, 2tl, 12–13; StockImageFactory.com/Shutterstock, 2tr, 8–9 (boy); AlexandrMusuc/Shutterstock, 2ml, 6–7; Andersen Ross Photography Inc/Getty, 2mr, 14–15; airdone/iStock, 2bl, 10–11 (girl); VisualCommunications/iStock, 2br, 3; Jana Ščigelová/Dreamstime, 4–5; rukxstockphoto/Shutterstock, 8–9 (background); Pla2na/Shutterstock, 10–11 (background); Designs Stock/Shutterstock, 16tl; boommaval/Shutterstock, 16tr; Davydenko Yuliia/Shutterstock, 16bl; Yeti studio/Shutterstock, 16br.

Library of Congress Cataloging-in-Publication Data
Names: Nilsen, Genevieve, author.
Title: Taste / by Genevieve Nilsen.
Description: Minneapolis, MN: Jump!, Inc., (2023)
Series: My senses | Includes index.
Audience: Ages 3–6
Identifiers: LCCN 2022011558 (print)
LCCN 2022011559 (ebook)
ISBN 9798885240956 (hardcover)
ISBN 9798885240963 (paperback)
ISBN 9798885240970 (ebook)
Subjects: LCSH: Taste—Juvenile literature.
Classification: LCC QP456 .N55 2023 (print) | LCC QP456 (ebook) | DDC 612.8/7—dc23/eng/20220325
LC record available at https://lccn.loc.gov/2022011558
LC ebook record available at https://lccn.loc.gov/2022011559

MY SENSES

TASTE

by Genevieve Nilsen

TABLE OF CONTENTS

Words to Know 2

Taste 3

Let's Review! 16

Index 16

WORDS TO KNOW

candy

salty

sour

sweet

taste

tongue

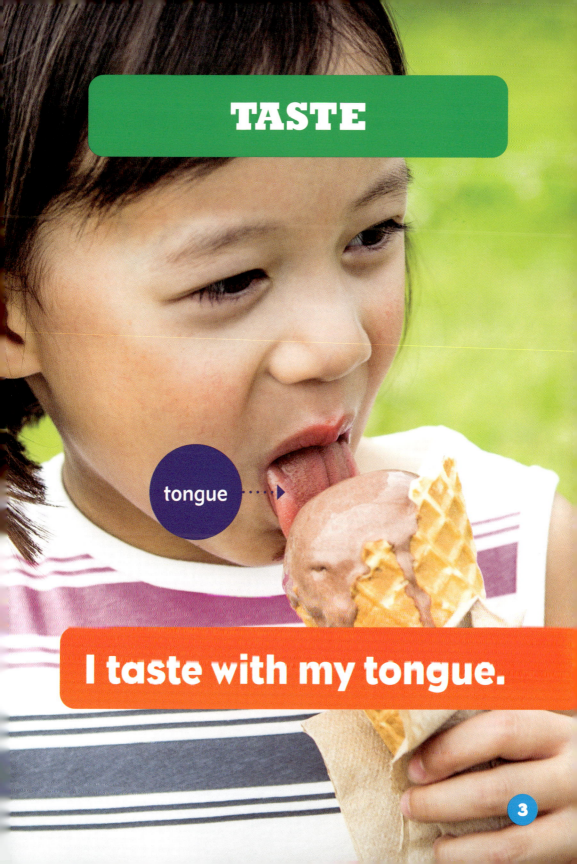

pickle

I eat a pickle.

It tastes sour.

I eat a lemon.

They taste salty.

It tastes salty.

It tastes sweet.

cake

We eat cake.

LET'S REVIEW!

We use our tongues to taste. Have you ever tasted the foods below? Were they sweet, sour, or salty?

INDEX

eat 4, 6, 8, 10, 12, 14
salty 9, 11
sour 5, 7

sweet 13, 15
taste 3, 5, 7, 9, 11, 13, 15
tongue 3